Hacking For Beginners

Everything You Need To Know To Become An Elite Hacker

Dexter Silverstein

Table of Contents

Introduction

Welcome to the wonderful world of hacking, a seemingly magical world, crafted out of the heart of mystery and wonder, but an oh so very real world where those who hesitate for even just a moment end up in very deep doo-doo, and only the elite have what it takes to survive!

This book explains everything you need to know in order to set you on the path toward becoming an elite hacker. I will assume that you are completely capable of working a computer and know how to use certain basic applications such as a browser and something like notepad.

However, you will need to learn to do other things as you progress through the lessons in this book, unless you happen to already know them.

This book also recommends that you engage in networking activity inside the hacking community and forge strong relationships with like-minded hackers, though it isn't necessary to succeed as a hacker and entirely optional. However, communication with other hackers would help a great deal to speed up your learning curve and help to ensure that you become an elite hacker.

Ethically speaking, hacking is not good or bad, but rather is a very pure and objective science, and thus this book aims to take a neutral perspective on hacking.

Please note, that some of the steps detailed in this book aren't necessary for you to follow. However, I fully recommend you do follow all the steps to a tee, because they'll provide you with the foundation you need in order to later evolve into a well-rounded elite hacker.

In order to complete this book, you need nothing more than a computer, an Internet connection, and the drive to become an elite hacker.

Disclaimer

This book will NOT teach you how to do anything illegal, and the author highly recommends you stay within the bounds of the law. This book is simply a beginner's guide to hacking which will teach you what you need to do in order to become an elite hacker. The decisions you make on what kind of elite hacker you want to become is solely up to you. The author of this guide encourages you to become a good and ethical hacker, but it's ultimately your choice which path you decide to go down.

If you decide to get into something illegal, this book shall bear no responsibility for your actions. Lastly, this book nor the author will be held responsible for any damages that may be incurred from following this guide. Everything that this book teaches is purely for informational purposes and any implementation is completely at your own risk with the responsibility being solely on your own shoulders.

How To Become A Hacker

Hackers, they were and will always be greatly feared by anyone who dares to touch any piece of technology. Politicians, celebrities, corporations, or just about anyone or any entity can get hacked. But what actually is a hacker? And what exactly is their motivation to hack?

There is a common misconception that all hackers are criminals and should be locked up. However, this is not always the case. Hackers have created some of the most amazing pieces of software the tech-industry has ever known. Maybe you didn't even know that the person who created that piece of software you use every day and absolutely love is actually a hacker, or was at one time a hacker. Is a hacker, was a hacker, it's all the same, because once you become a hacker, once you see the treasure that lies at the very bottom of the rabbit hole, you can never go back, unless perhaps your memory were to be erased, but even then your reputation would proceed you, and well … we're getting ahead of ourselves here.

Anyway, some of the most well-known, most reputable individuals in the tech industry were once hackers, I'm talking greats like Steve Jobs, Bill Gates, and a plethora of others. You see, many a hacker has made it to the top of their industry, and they didn't do it the fair way exactly, if you know what I mean. Well, perhaps you don't know what I mean. Pay it no mind. It's fine. We're fine. You're fine. Just forget I even mentioned that. Where were we? Oh yes ...

You can basically put all hackers into two different camps, the black-hat, and the white-hat. The black-hat are the bad ones you hear about, the ones who want to steal your credit card number,, personal information and completely wipe out your entire savings. They are the bad guys, so to speak. The white-hat, on the other hand are the good guys, they hack for good, test security systems, and create some very fine works of code.

There are some hackers who refer to themselves as grey-hat, but don't trust those, they're really just black-hat trying to put a spin on things to confuse you.

That leads me into the most frequently asked question about hackers, which is: why do hackers hack?

The answer is almost as simple as the question, because they can. You see, hackers like to test boundaries, they like to test what they can or can't do. The objectives between the black-hat and the white-hat tends to differ a little though. Black-hat generally has no regard for the law or others, it is a dark path indeed. White-hat, on the other hand, have good intentions and are usually quite sincere, at least they seem to have good intentions and be sincere, but we don't really know what's actually going on with them.

You have to be careful though, because even if you set out to be white hat, the black hat will try to turn you, they'll try to draw you in and make you see the power of the black hat, and vice-versa. It can really be quite the conundrum when you're confused about which side you're on.

Chapter 1: The Foundation

The foundation is extremely important to get right if you're a beginner. It doesn't matter what you think you know about hacking, you must start at the foundation. You can't build a house from the roof down. And in the case of hacking, you will need to build a foundation before you can even dream of beginning to hack. Well, you could dream about it if you really wanted to. Anyway, that's what we're going to learn in this chapter, the foundation!

In this chapter, you learn what operating system to use, and what kind of computer and programming languages you'll need to learn in order to become a hacker.

Requirements:
- A PC (personal computer) with or without windows
- An internet connection

Operating System

The recommended OS (operating system) you'll need for your hacking activities is Linux. Linux is an open-source operating system which is ready for download for everyone with an internet connection. This OS is difficult to install and so it's highly recommended that you search on Linux forums for any help you might need to install it.

The advantage of installing Linux is that you can run it alongside Windows on the same computer. If you use Windows alone, you can't hack properly. A Macintosh also should not be used because the architecture of MacOS is similarly difficult to hack with. Also, a Mac simply isn't capable of running an OS like Linux properly, well it could be doable, but since you're not a real hacker yet, it would be a real challenge for you to get Linux running on a Mac, so go with a PC.

Before you install Linux, you have to decide which version of Linux you want to install. Some versions of Linux are unstable, others are stable but don't work so well (long story), and others are just really difficult to understand. Thus, the recommended version of Linux that you should install is Ubuntu Linux, a simple, stable version with nearly endless possibilities for all of your hacking endeavors. Ubuntu is also as user-friendly and easy to understand as it gets with Linux, which really just makes Ubuntu the perfect version of Linux for you. However, the choice is really up to you, if you feel like it you can choose one of the many other versions of Linux. But don't say I didn't warn you when you're so frustrated that things won't work that you accidentally decide the take a baseball bat to your computer and smash it to little tiny bits.

HTML

If you didn't learn a programming language yet, this

book recommends that you learn the basics of HTML (HyperText Markup Language) as a first step. HTML is the markup language behind numerous websites, and is an essential language for all hackers to know. But why really learn HTML? HTML is a really simple, really basic language to learn, and is a first step toward becoming a hacker. I mean if you can't even figure out a super basic markup language like HTML, then how do you ever expect to become a hacker? You must learn HTML! And once you do learn HTML, besides being one step closer to being a hacker, you'll also have the added benefit of being able to create a website if you wanted to.

But just learning the basics of HTML is only the start, you need to become a pro at HTML. You need to really understand how one line of markup affects another and vice versa. If you can figure out HTML, you are ready for the next step, which is to learn an actual real programming language. Yes, HTML is not actually a programming language, nonetheless, you still need it.

Tip:
Look at different sites and view their HTML code, because you can learn a lot analyzing HTML code. Some sites use basic HTML and other use HTML5. Check the code of all sites you visit. And when you're analyzing the HTML of a site, try to understand relate to what lines of HTML code relate to which elements on the site, so that you can understand how the site was built.

Perl

Perl is a Unix-based programming language. It possesses a few elements of C and other Unix-Based languages. Perl isn't the most difficult language to learn, and its basic elements overlap with many other programming languages. This is a big advantage, because if you know Perl, then most other programming languages aren't so difficult to learn. However, Perl uses a lot of non-alphanumeric characters, which makes it difficult to understand. This is why most of hackers don't learn Perl at all. Still, it is worth learning as a first programming language, because it's perhaps one of the easiest languages to learn, and learning it will allow you to learn other languages more easily. You don't have to master it, you just have to get the basics down.

PHP

PHP is an extremely popular programming language, also known as a server-side scripting language, because it's basically made for creating dynamic Web pages. PHP was inspired by Perl, works similarly to Perl, as well as Python (don't worry, we'll get to Python). Some advantages of PHP is that it is not that hard to learn, and pretty darn powerful, which is why most hackers know PHP. It's recommended to invest a lot of time learning PHP if you want to learn other more advanced programming languages later on. However, learning PHP is not a requirement to become an elite hacker. Still, if you're coming from nothing, you should definitely learn

PHP.

IP Address

IP, in this case, stands for Internet Protocol. And an IP address is basically a numerical string that identifies where your Internet connection is coming from. This number lets other computers know exactly where you are. Your IP address can be changed if you wanted to change it. For example, if you want to have it look as if you're at a computer located in China, you can set this up using a nifty little piece of software called a VPN (virtual private network). If you search for VPNs in any search engine, you can find a large selection of both free and paid VPNs. Try setting up a few VPNs and changing your IP address to get better acquainted with this concept. The ability to change one's IP address is a skill that you'll definitely need to become good at if you are ever to become an elite hacker.

Python, C, and C++

If you understand HTML and Perl or PHP, then you are ready for some more advanced programming languages like Python, C, or C++. Some of these languages are harder to learn than others, just like real languages.

The easiest one to learn is Python. Python is straightforward, logical, and as a result, makes it a great programming language to learn for inexperienced hackers. Since Python is straightforward, lots of people use it and so there is a lot of information out there about it. The internet is full of tutorials on how to write a good Python code, these kinds of tutorials are especially useful for up and coming hackers. Python is thus a great language to learn to become a hacker and knowing it alone is enough to be a hacker, and perhaps all you'll ever need.

However, if you like challenges (which hackers usually do), you can also decide to learn a more difficult programming language like C. C is not as easy and understandable as HTML, Perl, PHP or Python, but it can help you to create more complex programs. If you know C, you are then a position to learn C++, an even more difficult programming language than C, which can give you even more amazing results. However, there are disadvantages with both C and C++, such as that the debugging of your code can take a long time if you're inexperienced, time which you cannot afford to lose as a hacker. Therefore, these languages are not suitable for inexperienced hackers. So if at all in doubt, just go with Python, and you can always learn C later if you still wanted to.

Chapter 2: Your First Friend

Your first friend as a hacker will be Stack Overflow, you find it at Stackoverflow.com (that's s t a c k o v e r f l o w dot com).

You can go here and ask questions regarding anything related to programming, and you'll get answers fairly quickly.

It's a large community. Most of the community members are programmers, and some of those programmers are hackers, and their forums are all searchable, so it's a great place to acquire a ton of knowledge.

As you progress from beginner to advanced hacker, at one point you'll be the one on the other side answering other people's questions.

Anyway, this website is so valuable, that it's really critical you get familiar with it and so I thought it was deserving of its own chapter. Seriously, this is the ultimate community on the Internet that you want to be a part of.

Therefore, treat Stack Overflow well, and go on it often, because it is, from this day forward, your new best friend.

Chapter 3: Hacker Lifestyle

Hacking is not just a thing you do, hacking is a lifestyle. This chapter covers what you need to do in order to live the lifestyle.

Mindset

First things first, you've got to get the mindset if a hacker down. Hackers enjoy solving problems. While many people will shy away from problems or would rather live a life without problems, that is not the way of a hacker. A hacker can't stand a life without problems, as hackers love problems. If there is no problem to tackle, if there is nothing to solve, then a hacker feels bored, empty, and without purpose.

A hacker would rather be tackling a problem than doing anything else. The high of solving problems is the hacker's purpose. If a problem seems impossible to solve, all the better. There is nothing that a hacker loves more than tackling the impossible! Because hackers make the impossible possible, that is what a hacker does!

If there is something that can't be penetrated, some coding issue that can't be debugged. The hacker's eyes light up, and the hacker focuses relentlessly until the problem gets solved.

No problem is too great for a hacker, no wall is too high, no piece of code too complex, there is always a way, always another angle that can worked.

This is the mindset of a hacker!

Friends

Hackers have only 5 friends, their computer, their programming books, Stackoverflow.com, their fingerless gloves, and other hackers.

Hackers will go out of their way to do anything for their hacker friends. And when you make some hacker friends, it's not uncommon for them to knock on your window in the middle of the night because they need your help with something. You might be tempted to try to convince yourself that you're just dreaming and go back to sleep. You're not just dreaming, your hacker friend is at the window! So slap yourself awake and go on over and open the window to let your friend in.

Clothes

As a hacker, fashion is not such a big thing. But it's best if you dress the part. You'll need weird looking T-shirts that separate yourself from common people, thin high-tech looking jeans with fashionable rips in them, a good high-tech looking jacket, some fingerless gloves, cool shades that you can wear even at night and still see, and a laptop case with shoulder strap. On your feet, running shoes or running sneakers are best, because you never know when it'll be time to run. Sometimes a hacker just has those moments where running is, well, necessary.

Jewelry

Hackers do not wear any jewelry unless it's high-tech, think touchscreen watches and multifunction vibrating bracelets. A pendant or amulet on a thin chain around the neck would also be acceptable.

Hairstyle

Hackers don't leave their hair a mess. Having a sleek looking hairstyle is important. If you don't have hair, that's fine. But if you do have hair, best if you put some gel in it and push it back or spike it. Or if you have curly hair, then curly hair is fine, just make sure it's well trimmed. If your hair is long, then cut it shorter.

Favorite Color

The favorite color of a hacker is most always black. Blue, red, green, or orange also make acceptable favorite colors. Never yellow, purple or pink.

Conventions

It is important that hackers go to conventions to meet other hackers. Sci-Fi conventions, Tech conventions, Programming conventions, and of course Hacking conventions are all acceptable. Be sure to get out there and go to a convention at least once every few months, and try to find and identify other hackers, just look for the fingerless gloves, and start the conversation by talking about debugging issues or something of that nature.

Chapter 4: Become An Elite Hacker

As a hacker, you must be dedicated. But to become an elite hacker you have to solve many problems and win the respect of your peers. If you don't have peers yet, then you had better go to more conventions and get on Stack Overflow a bit more.

Write open-source software

Write a funny or useful program and share the program and the code with your network of hackers. If any of them voluntarily improves the code, then you know that you have found one who can be trusted.

Help to test and debugging programs

Beta-testers are the most important group of people you can use to improve your programs (before 'official' release) and give feedback on their experience with the program. If you have some bugs in your freshly made program, your beta-testers can find them and can possibly tell you how to fix them.

You can also become a beta-tester. All you have to do is test some programs that other hackers have created, and help them make a better version. Just search through forums for programs that other hackers have shared with each other, and try the program out, and then provide your feedback. The other hacker will appreciate your feedback. Now they're more likely to help you should you need feedback for one of your programs.

Share useful information

Search forums for questions and either find the right answer or give them a push in the right direction. Most people will appreciate it and you will gather some more respect from the community.

Volunteer

If you want to volunteer to help the community, you will earn a lot of respect. The hacker community is built and maintained by volunteers. So it's highly recommended that you ask around if there are any projects that you can assist with. If you volunteer to assist in projects often, you'll make a name for yourself, and you'll learn a lot in the process.

How long to become an elite hacker?
There is no specified period of time that it will take you to become an elite hacker. It largely all depends on you fast you learn, how many other hackers you network with, and how big of a name you are able to build for yourself.

Chapter 5: A Word of Caution

Whether you're on the path to becoming an elite hacker or if you're already an elite hacker, there will come a time when the other site will try to turn you. Now as this book is trying to promote well-intentioned ethical hacking, I'm not going to tell you what to do if the white-hat try to turn you.

However, if the black-hat try to turn you there is only so much you can do about it, and very few places you can run to for help. Ultimately though, it's going to be your choice if you decide to give in to the temptation of the black-hat.

The power of the black-hat is quite strong, and how the black-hat will try to turn you will usually happen in a way that you least expect. Perhaps someone in your network is actually a black-hat, perhaps someone that you're very fond of. You never really know, as these things can come from out of nowhere. One day you're on your happy hacking journey, then next minute you find yourself in a battle over the fate of your soul.

I'm going to be completely honest with you here, the power of the black-hat is strong, so strong in fact that most don't have the power to resist. Thus, prevention is the best way.

So how does one prevent ever being put in a situation where the black-hat is trying to turn them in the first place? Constant vigilance is the only way. You see, once you go down the road of hacking, you can't really ever completely trust anyone. Thus, you should expect the worst, even from the best people.

You must always be watching, always be aware, both of the environment around you, as well as what's going on inside your computer. A threat could strike at any moment, and you must be prepared for such a threat. Because let's face it, when you're dealing with the black-hat, you're never truly actually safe. No conversation is actually ever private. Because the black-hat can see and hear all. The only truly safe place is the deep inner-recesses of your mind.

There is nothing further I can really say about it.

Thus, be vigilant, and be safe!

Conclusion

You have now learned the basics of how to become a hacker. You know what operating system to use, the basic programming languages to learn and the skills that require you to become a successful hacker. There is only one thing left to say in this book, and that is Good luck! Because now you are armed with a clear path to becoming an elite hacker, which is far more than this author had when he started.